THE CROCHET WORKSHOP

learn to crochet in quick and easy steps

Emma Osmond

SEARCH PRESS

CONTENTS

NOTE: *Emma has used Rowan yarns for all the projects in the book, but these can be substituted with any yarn of a similar weight. Always test the gauge (tension) before starting a project, whichever yarn you use (see page 8).*

INTRODUCTION

///

My name is Emma Osmond. I am a mobile consultant for Rowan Yarns and a 'crazed' knitwear and crochet designer. Needlecraft was my hobby from a young age, taught to me by my grandmother and, today, it has now become my career.

I worked at Liberty of London in the haberdashery department and just fell in love with the beautiful yarn Rowan produce. I was lucky enough to teach a number of beginner crochet and knitting classes in Liberty of London, which were aimed at 'time-poor' career people, who may have learnt the craft when they were younger and just needed a slight confidence boost; as well as those who just want to make something handmade for themselves or their homes.

My designs are simplistic, but focus around a modern lifestyle. When I learnt to crochet it was something that took me by complete surprise. I was amazed at how calming and rewarding crochet can be – I was immediately 'hooked'.

My theory is that if you learn the basics, and can understand the process, then crochet is very simple and your finished pieces will have that 'wow' factor.

Follow me on my crochet workshop journey. I will start by teaching you how to find the right hook so you can quickly progress from a simple chain to producing some beautiful projects for yourself, your home or to share as gifts.

Emma x

Crochet is quick, easy and fun to learn, enabling you to create simple yet stylish pieces for yourself and your home in no time.

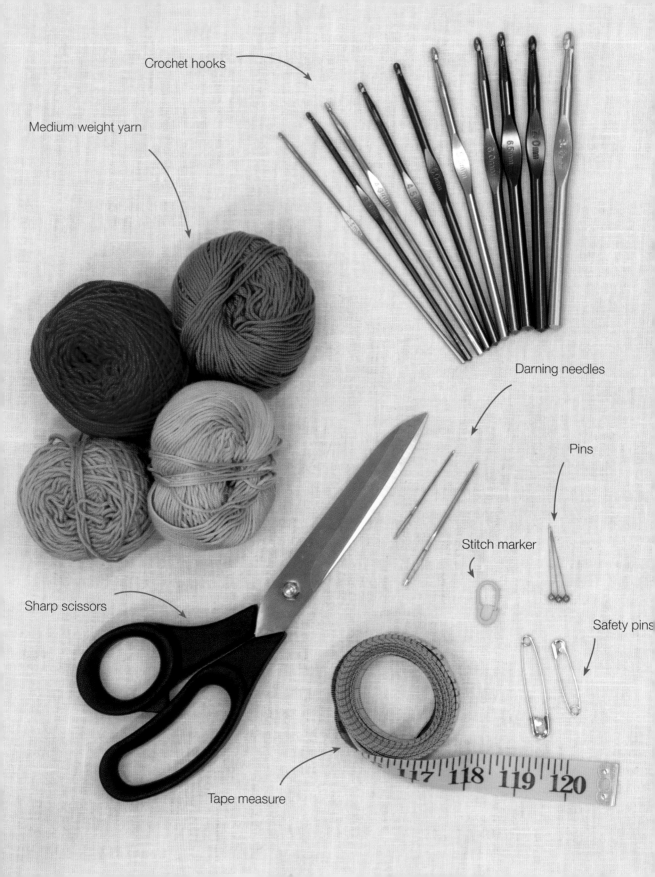

Crochet hooks

Medium weight yarn

Darning needles

Pins

Stitch marker

Sharp scissors

Safety pins

Tape measure

117 118 119 120

BASIC EQUIPMENT

One of the great things about crochet is that you need very few things to get going – just a crochet hook and some yarn and you are ready to go!

Like knitting needles, crochet hooks come in various sizes – all measured by the diameter of the hook. You will often find the size stamped on the flat thumb rest area around the middle of the hook. Hooks come in wood, plastic or metal and are also available with soft grip handles – which are popular for those with arthritis, or who find their hands tire during longer crochet sessions.

The size of the hook, as well as the yarn you use with it, will determine the size of the stitches it produces. The most common hook sizes are US B/1–L/11 (2.25–8mm), but finer hooks are used for more intricate lace crochet work.

Most beginners will start with a US size G/6 or H/8 (4 or 5mm) hook and a medium weight yarn, but for other projects see the chart in the yarn section on the next page for a guide as to which hook to use with which yarn weight.

OTHER EQUIPMENT:
I like to keep some items from my sewing basket handy, such as a pair of sharp scissors, a large darning needle, pins, safety pins and finally, a tape measure.

CROCHET HOOK SIZES AND CONVERSIONS

US SIZES	METRIC SIZES (mm)
-	2.0
B/1	2.25
-	2.5
C/2	2.75
-	3.0
D/3	3.25
E/4	3.5
F/5	3.75
G/6	4.0
7	4.5
H/8	5.0
I/9	5.5
J/10	6.0
K/10½	6.5
-	7.0
L/11	8.0
M/13	9.0
N/15	10.0

YARN

It is important that you take plenty of time to choose the correct yarn and the best accompanying hook for your project. Yarns come in many different types and are available in a dazzling array of thicknesses, weights, colours and textures.

Usually the weight or type of yarn is printed on the label – also known as the ball band. The label will tell you the weight of the yarn, the gauge (or tension), the washing instructions, and the most suitable hook size to use.

If you are making a project that uses more than one ball of yarn, you will also need to check the 'dye lot' number on the ball band to ensure that the colour will be exactly the same. Some dye lots can vary so dramatically that when made up, your piece will look striped, as if you have used two different colour shades.

If you can't match the dye lots or are working with hand-dyed yarn, you can work alternate rows from two balls of yarn to avoid the stripy effect.

Yarn weight category	Super fine	Fine	Light	Medium	Bulky	Super bulky
	1	2	3	4	5	6
Type of yarns in category	4-ply, Sock	Sport	DK	Worsted	Chunky	Bulky
	Fingering	Baby	Light	Afghan, Aran	Craft, Rug	Roving
Crochet gauge ranges. Measured in single crochet (UK double crochet) over 4in (10cm)	21-32 sts	16-20 sts	12-17 sts	11-14 sts	9-11 sts	6-9 sts
Recommended crochet hook in metric	2.25-3.5mm	3.5-4.5mm	4.5-5.5mm	5.5-6.5mm	6.5-9mm	9mm and larger
Recommended crochet hook in US size	Steel hooks, B/1 to E/4	E/4 to G/6	G/6 to J/9	J/9 to K/10½	K/10½ to M/N13	K/10½ to M/N13 and larger

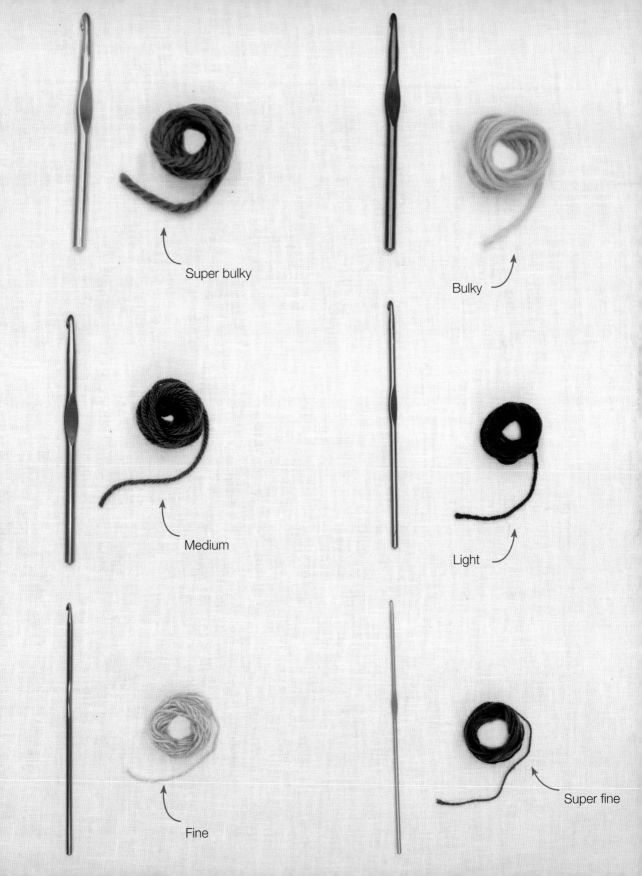

Super bulky

Bulky

Medium

Light

Fine

Super fine

THINGS YOU NEED TO KNOW

///////////////////////////////////

GAUGE (TENSION)

The size of crochet stitches is described as the gauge (or tension in the UK) to which they are worked. The gauge must be checked carefully before starting a design as you must work at the correct gauge in order to ensure the correct size of the finished piece.

MAKING A GAUGE SWATCH (TENSION SWATCH)

To make a gauge swatch, use the hook size, yarn and stitch indicated in the gauge section to make a small sample piece. In most cases this is measured over 4in (10cm) but you should always make a swatch slightly larger than this, as the edges of your work are liable to distort and can lead to an incorrect measurement.

ADJUSTING A GAUGE

If you find that you have more rows or stitches than the pattern suggests, then your gauge is too tight and you should switch to a larger hook. If there are fewer stitches or rows, then try switching to a smaller size hook. Continue to make swatches until you achieve the correct number of stitches to match the gauge.

MAKING A GAUGE SWATCH

ONE. Using the crochet hook, yarn and stitches specified for the project, make a gauge swatch, then use a tape measure to measure 4in (10cm) horizontally across the square. Mark this length with a pin at each end.

TWO. Do the same vertically. Count the number of stitches and rows between the pins.

UNDERSTANDING STITCHES

Whilst there are many crochet stitches you will eventually learn, the most common are shown below. Essentially, each stitch is made by forming a loop of yarn and drawing this loop through existing loops. It really is much more straightforward then you might think.

Single crochet
(double crochet UK)

Half double crochet
(half treble crochet UK)

Double crochet
(treble crochet UK)

US/UK CROCHET TERMS

Crochet terms in the US are different from the UK; the most common confusion arises when the same term is used to refer to completely different things. I have written this book using US terminology first, with the UK equivalent in brackets.

The table to the right shows the conversions.

US		UK	
Slip stitch	ss	Slip stitch	ss
Single crochet	sc	Double crochet	dc
Half double crochet	hdc	Half treble crochet	htr
Double crochet	dc	Treble crochet	tr
Treble crochet	tr	Double treble crochet	dtr

ABBREVIATIONS

Written patterns contain many abbreviations. These can differ depending upon whether you are following a US or UK pattern; always check the given abbreviations to make sure that you have understood the instruction. Because this book has been written to help you get started with understanding the stitches and without the need to worry about abbreviations, all of my patterns are written in long hand.

beg	beginning		inc	increase
CC	contrast colour		m	metre(s)
ch	chain		MB	make bobble
ch-sp	chain space		MC	main colour
cm	centimetre(s)		mm	millimetre(s)
corner-sp	corner space		rem	remain(ing)
dc	double crochet		RS	right side
dctog	double crochet two stitches together (decrease by one stitch)		sp	space
dec	decrease		ss	slip stitch
dk	double knit (yarn weight)		st(s)	stitch(es)
dtr	double treble		tr	treble
g	gram(s)		tr2tog	treble two stitches together (decrease by one stitch)
hdc	half double crochet		trtr	treble treble
htr	half treble		WS	wrong side
in	inch(es)		yd	yard(s)

CROCHET BASICS

In this section, I will guide you through all of the basic skills needed to crochet. From holding your yarn and hook to starting a foundation chain, single crochet (UK double crochet), half double crochet (UK half treble crochet), double crochet (UK treble crochet), treble crochet (UK double treble crochet) and creating slip stitches.

We will then move onto cover turning chains, joining in a new colour, shaping and joining pieces together.

HOLDING THE HOOK

There are different ways of holding the crochet hook. You will need to experiment and find the way that feels the most comfortable for you. If your hand isn't comfortable, it will cramp up and your stitches will not be even.

The position I recommend is similar to holding a pencil. Hold the crochet hook as you would a pencil with your thumb and index finger on the thumb grip.

HOLDING THE YARN

To produce good crochet you will need to get an even gauge (tension). Your left hand plays the main role in achieving this. Holding the yarn correctly will enable you to get a good gauge to your crochet.

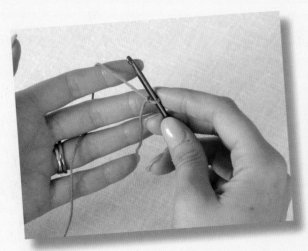

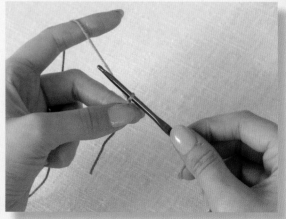

ONE: to tension your yarn, using your left hand, take the yarn between your middle and ring finger and up over the top of your index finger.

TWO: take the tail end of the yarn between your left thumb and middle finger, close your two smaller fingers to tension your yarn and you are ready to crochet!

MAKING A SLIP KNOT

There are many ways to make a slip knot. This is the way I teach new crocheters as it is simple and easy to learn. You want to make sure you can alter the length by pulling on the tail end of the finished slip knot.

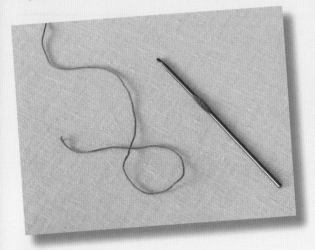

ONE: using ball end of yarn, cross over the tail end.

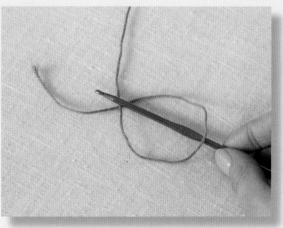

TWO: take the hook and place it under the loop.

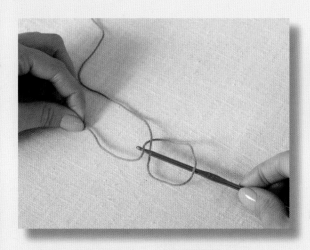

THREE: while holding the tail end of the yarn, slip the hook under the tail end and catch the yarn.

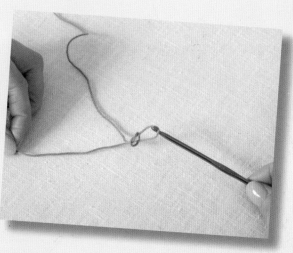

FOUR: bring the hook back, catching the yarn and pulling through the loop.

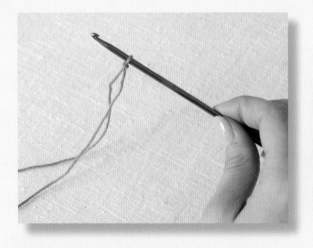

TIP

You want to make sure your slip knot is 'snug' on your hook, not too loose, but also not too tight.

FIVE: pull the tail end to tighten the loop on the hook.

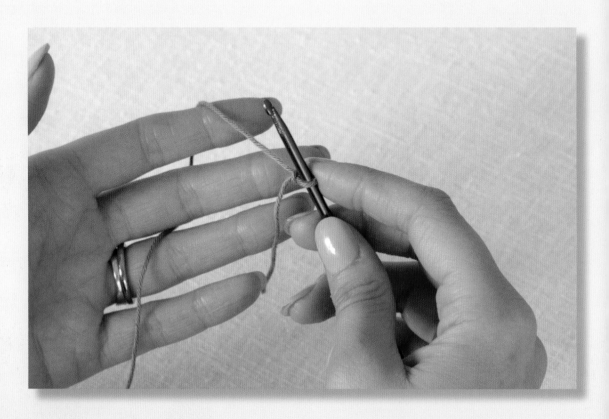

FOUNDATION CHAIN

The foundation chain is the start of most crochet projects. From pillows to sweaters this is how it all starts. I suggest making long foundation chains to perfect your technique, as being quick at forming a good foundation chain will speed up your completion time on projects.

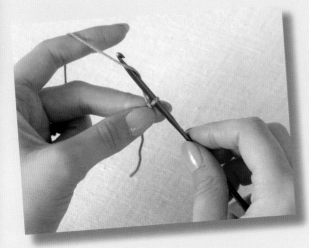

ONE: with your slip knot on the hook and the yarn in your left hand ready, place the hook under the yarn.

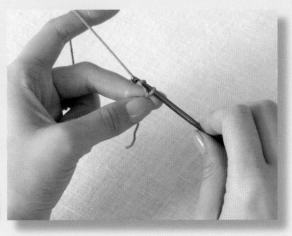

TWO: using the hook, bring the yarn through the slip knot. You will need to have the hook facing downwards so as to not catch it on the loop.

THREE: continue to bring the yarn all the way through the slip knot.

FOUR: repeat this step for the length of foundation chain required.

SINGLE CROCHET (UK DOUBLE CROCHET)

The single crochet (abbreviated in patterns as sc, or dc in the UK) is one of the most common crochet stitches. A fabric made of all single crochet stitches is fairly dense and solid, making it perfect for cosy shawls, afghans, place mats or any number of home decor items.

ONE: insert the hook into the stitch that you want to work.

TWO: take the hook under the yarn.

THREE: pull the hook back through the first loop on the hook (two loops on hook).

FOUR: take the hook under the yarn again.

When working in single crochet (UK double crochet), twist the hook so that the hook faces downwards when drawing through the two loops on the hook. This will stop it catching.

FIVE: pull the hook back through both of the remaining loops on the hook.

Here is a finished sample worked in single crochet (UK double crochet).

HALF DOUBLE CROCHET (UK HALF TREBLE CROCHET)

The half double crochet (UK half treble crochet) is half way between single crochet and double crochet (or between a double crochet and treble crochet in the UK). It produces a firm and durable fabric and is used in many patterns and motifs.

ONE: wrap the hook under the yarn.

TWO: insert the hook into the stitch that you want to work.

THREE: take the hook under the yarn and back through the first loop on the hook (three loops on hook).

FOUR: take the hook under the yarn and bring through all three stitches at once.

TIP

Pulling through three loops at once can be a little tricky at first. You can go through one loop at a time, but just remember not to catch the yarn whilst doing this.

FIVE: this is how the finished stitch should look.

Here is a finished sample worked in half double crochet.

DOUBLE CROCHET (UK TREBLE CROCHET)

Double crochet (UK treble crochet) produces a more open fabric. The finished stitches are tall, so can produce a speedy result.

ONE: place the hook under the yarn and insert the hook into the stitch that you want to work.

TWO: wrap the hook under the yarn again and come through the stitch (three loops on hook).

THREE: wrap the yarn under the hook again and pull through the first two loops, wrap the yarn under the hook and pull through the remaining two loops.

FOUR: this is how the finished stitch should look.

Here is a finished sample worked in double crochet.

SLIP STITCH

The slip stitch is used to move along your work and to join rounds. It is used a lot when working motifs.

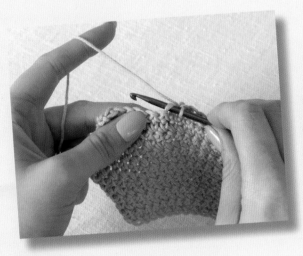

ONE: insert the hook into the next stitch.

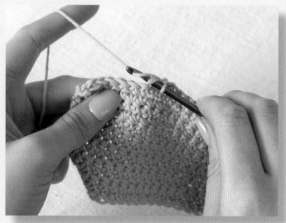

TWO: wrap the yarn under the hook.

THREE: bring through both stitches on the hook. You have now completed a slip stitch.

WORKING ON A FLAT PIECE - TURNING CHAIN

When working in rows or rounds of crochet, you will need to make a chain which is long enough to take you to the height of the next row before continuing with your chosen stitches. If you are working on a flat piece of work, the chains are created at the end of your row before you turn your work. These are called turning chains. Each stitch has a suggested number of chains which will take your hook to the correct height.

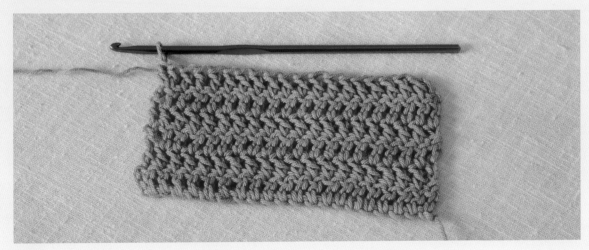

ONE: above shows a piece of work before commencing a turning chain.

US	UK	Chains required
Single	Double	1
Half Double	Half Treble	2
Double	Treble	3
Treble	Double Treble	4

TWO: make the required number of chains at the end of the row.

As I have been working in double crochet (UK treble), I have made three chains. At the end of each row you will need to work into the top of the turning chain on the previous row to complete your final stitch.

JOINING IN A NEW YARN COLOUR

There are many ways of adding a new colour to your work. These will vary depending on the type of stitch you are using. The slip stitch can be used for any stitch, but is best worked at the beginning of the row and not when working in the round. Here, I am working in single crochet (UK double crochet).

ONE: work until you are on the last stitch of the row. Work your stitch in the normal way until you get to the last step of your stitch (two loops on the hook). Take the new yarn you wish to use, make it into a loop and slip it onto the hook.

TWO: bring the new yarn through the two loops to complete a single crochet (UK double crochet).

THREE: turn and continue to work your stitches. Cut the first yarn and knot together the two ends. You will need to sew in these ends once your project is completed.

INCREASING

When making a garment or following a pattern, you may need to add stitches. This can be done in the middle or at the end of the row; both ways are done in the same way. Here, I am working in single crochet (UK double crochet).

ONE: work one complete stitch.

TWO: insert the hook into the same space or stitch below and work another stitch.

THREE: this is how the finished increase stitch should look.

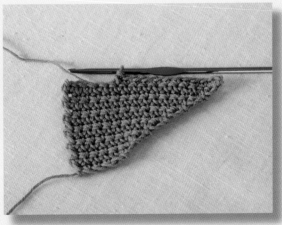

THREE: your work should look similar to this if you increase on every row.

DECREASING

As with increasing, when making a garment or following a pattern you may need to remove stitches. Again, it can be worked at any point during a row. As before, I am working in single crochet (UK double crochet).

ONE: work your stitch to the last step (two loops on the hook).

TWO: work a single crochet (UK double crochet) into the next stitch, up to the last step again (three loops on hook).

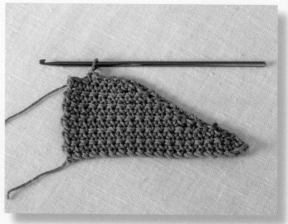

THREE: complete the decrease by bringing the yarn through all the loops on the hook.

FOUR: your work should look similar to this if you decrease on every row.

JOINING TWO PIECES TOGETHER - USING MATTRESS STITCH

You can use a variety of sewn stitches to join your crochet pieces. First, sew all yarn ends in neatly and block pieces if necessary before assembling them. Use a large darning needle to stitch with.

ONE: lay the two pieces next to each other, right sides up.

TWO: insert the needle from back to front in the first stitch on the right-hand side and then the same on the left-hand side.

THREE: insert the needle back into the right-hand side piece of work and up one stitch.

FOUR: repeat on the left-hand side and continue up like a ladder.

FIVE: pull tight every few rows to make a nice invisible seam.

FIVE: when you have worked across the whole length you will have a nice invisible seam like above.

JOINING TWO PIECES TOGETHER - CROCHET

A variation of the single crochet (UK double crochet) stitch can also be used to join together crochet pieces once complete. This can produce a firm and well-defined edge.

ONE: hold the two pieces you wish to join with right sides together.

TWO: insert the hook through both pieces of the work into the two corresponding stitches of the front and back pieces.

THREE: catch the yarn with the hook and bring it through the two pieces.

FOUR: insert the hook into the next stitch and catch the yarn to bring it through the two pieces (two loops on the hook).

FIVE: bring the first stitch through the second stitch (one loop remains). To continue along your work repeat steps 2-5 until you reach the end.

SIX: when you reach the end of your piece, you will need to fasten off to secure your work. To fasten off, you simply pull the tail end of the yarn through the loop on the hook.

//

NEXT STEPS

In this section I will guide you through how to make a ring, working stitches into a ring, missing stitches and working into a chain space. These stitches are most commonly used when creating crochet motifs.

//

MAKING A RING

Many crochet motifs are created by working in the round; starting at the centre and working outwards.

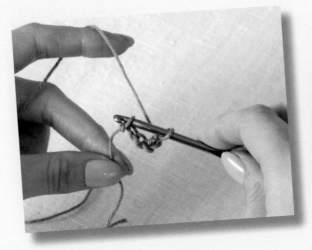

ONE: to make a ring, start by making a chain (in this shot I have made five chains).

TWO: join the ring using a slip stitch into the first chain from the slip knot.

THREE: here is how the finished ring should look.

WORKING STITCHES INTO A RING

Moving on from the ring, you will need to start working stitches into the centre.

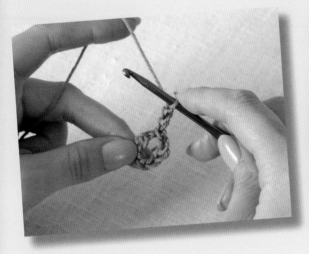

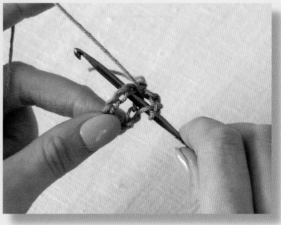

ONE: work the required number of chains to create the height of the stitch you wish to work. In this instance, we will be using double crochet (UK treble crochet) so I have made three chains.

TWO: to work the stitches simply place the hook into the centre of the ring and work a double crochet (UK treble crochet). Continue working double crochet (UK treble crochet) into the centre ring as required.

THREE: this is how your work should look as you continue to work double crochet (UK treble crochet) into the ring.

MISSING STITCHES

One of crochet's most recognisable characteristics is its use of decorative and open stitches. In some patterns you may be asked to skip one or more stitches. This creates a chain space.

ONE: complete the round by joining using slip stitch into the top of the third chain from the first round.

TWO: make five chains; this is the base of your chain space for the next round.
Usually your pattern will tell you the number of stitches required.

THREE: when working in the round you are sometimes asked to miss a stitch. In this example it shows missing two stitches and entering the third stitch (this makes a chain space).

WORKING INTO A CHAIN SPACE

You may find that you are asked to work a stitch, or a group of stitches, into a space created on the previous row or round, as opposed to working into a stitch.

ONE: when working into a chain space, you simply insert the hook into the large area underneath the chain of the previous round. Here we are working single crochet (UK double crochet), so you will need to make one chain in order to gain the height and then a series of single crochet (UK double crochet) stitches into the chain space.

TWO: this is how your work should look once you have worked eight stitches into a chain space.

PROJECTS

Using the skills you have learned in the previous sections, you will be able to follow these simple and stylish projects.

All of the patterns are written out in full, without any abbreviations, to help you get to grips with how patterns are structured and to gain quick results with your new skills.

STRIPED BOLSTER PILLOW

Add comfort to your lounge or bedroom with a beautiful handmade bolster pillow. Designed with a simple stripe that can be created in colours to match your home and big enough to be a feature on its own, or mixed with other pillows.

MATERIALS

Rowan Cocoon
2 x 3.5oz (100g), or any bulky
weight yarn

Photographed in A Shale 804
and B Scree 803

Hook: US K10½ (6.5mm)

Bolster pillow: 17¾ x 6¾in
(45cm x 17cm)

GAUGE

10 stitches and 6 rows measure
4in (10cm) over pattern using
K10½ (6.5mm) crochet hook

FINISHED SIZE

Length: 17¾in (45cm)
Width: 6¾in (17cm)

STRIPED BOLSTER PILLOW

MAIN SECTION
Make 47 chains with yarn A.

Row 1: Work first double crochet (UK treble crochet) into
the third chain from the hook. Work a double crochet (UK
treble crochet) into each chain to complete your row.

Make one chain – this is your turning chain. Turn your work.

Row 2: Work one single crochet (UK double crochet) into
the next and every stitch to the end of the row.

Using the slip stitch method join in yarn B. Make three
chains – these are your turning chains. Turn your work.

Row 3: Work one double crochet (UK treble crochet) into
next and every stitch to the end of the row.

Make one chain. Turn your work.

Row 4: Work one single crochet (UK double crochet) into
the next and every stitch to the end of the row.

Change to yarn A. Make three chains and turn your work.

Repeat the last two rows above changing colour every two
rows until work measures 23½in (60cm).

Fasten off.

TO MAKE THE ENDS
Using yarn A make 6 chains, join with a slip stitch.

Round 1: Make three chains, this is your first double
crochet (UK treble crochet). Work 15 more double crochet
(UK treble crochet) into the centre of the loop. You will have
16 stitches.

Join yarn B with slip stitch. Make three chains. Do not turn.
You are working in rounds.

Round 2: *Work one double crochet (UK treble crochet) into
next chain space. Work two doubles (UK treble crochet) into
the following chain space. Repeat from * seven more times.
You should have 25 stitches.

Join yarn A. Make three chains.

Round 3: Work one double crochet (UK treble crochet) into every stitch. You should have 25 stitches.

Join yarn B. Make three chains.

Round 4: *Work one double (UK treble crochet) into next chain space, work one double crochet (UK treble crochet) into following stitch. Repeat from * 24 times. Work final double crochet (UK treble crochet) into next chain space.

Fasten off.

Using yarn B make 6 chains, join with a slip stitch.

Round 1: Make three chains, this is your first double crochet (UK treble crochet), work 15 more double crochet (UK treble crochet) into the centre of the loop. You should have 16 stitches.

Join yarn A with slip stitch. Make three chains

Round 2: *Work one double crochet (UK treble crochet) into next chain space. Work two double crochets (UK treble crochet) into the following chain space. Repeat from * seven more times. You should have 25 stitches.

Join yarn B. Make three chains.

Round 3: Work one double crochet (UK treble crochet) into every stitch. You should have 25 stitches.

Join yarn A. Make three chains.

Round 4: *Work one double crochet (UK treble crochet) into next chain space, work one double crochet (UK treble crochet) into following stitch. Repeat from * 24 times. Work final double crochet (UK treble crochet) into next chain space.

Fasten off.

MAKING UP
Join main section widthways with mattress stitch. Insert your pillow pad. Attach each end piece.

TECHNIQUES USED

This project uses the following techniques:

Single crochet (UK double crochet) - *see page 18*

Double crochet (UK treble crochet)- *see page 22*

Next steps - *see page 33*

TASSEL SCARF

Get ready for winter with this universal scarf. Wrap it, tie it or simply drape it over your shoulders. A chunky feel with tassel detail makes this scarf a great addition to any outfit. Make it in a range of colours to enhance this simple, but elegant design.

MATERIALS

Rowan Big Wool
4 x 3.5oz (100g) balls, or any super bulky weight yarn

Photographed in Pantomime 79

Hook: US O16 (12mm)

GAUGE

7 stitches and 8 rows measures 4in (10cm) over single crochet (UK double crochet) pattern using O16 (12mm) crochet hook

FINISHED SIZE

Approximately 88 x 10in (223½ x 25cm) including tassels

TASSEL SCARF

Make 17 chains.

Row 1: Work first single crochet (UK double crochet) into the second chain from the hook. Work a single (UK double crochet) into each chain to the end of the row.
You should have 16 stitches.

Make one chain – this is your turning chain. Turn your work.

Row 2: Work a single crochet (UK double crochet) into the top of the second to last stitch of the previous row. Complete your row with single crochet (UK double crochet). Make one chain and turn your work.

Repeat the last row until your work measures 78in (198cm). Fasten off.

MAKING UP
For the tassels Cut sixty-four 20in (50cm) lengths of yarn. Group two lengths together and fold in half, insert the folded end into the first stitch at the base of the scarf. Pull halfway through. Pull the tail end through the loop made, pull to tighten. Repeat until you have a tassel on each stitch at the end of each row.

TECHNIQUES USED

This project uses the following techniques:

Single crochet (UK double crochet) - *see page 18*

SNUG COWL

A super snug cowl; simple yet effective. The chunky yarn and simple stitch make for a great texture and structure.

MATERIALS

Rowan Big Wool
2 x 3.5oz (100g) balls, or any super
bulky weight yarn

Photographed in Glum 056

Hook: US O16 (12mm)

GAUGE

7 stitches and 8 rows measures
4in (10cm) over single crochet (UK
double crochet) pattern using O16
(12mm) crochet hook

FINISHED SIZE

Approximately 39½ x 10in
(100 x 25cm)

SNUG COWL

Make 17 chains.

Row 1: Work first single crochet (UK double crochet) into
the second chain from the hook. Work a single crochet
(UK double crochet) into each stitch to the end of the row.
You should have 16 stitches.

Make one chain – this is your turning chain. Turn your work.

Row 2: Work a single crochet (UK double crochet) into
the top of the second to last stitch of the previous row.
Complete your row with single crochet (UK double crochet).
Make one chain and turn your work.

Repeat the last row until your work measures 39½in
(100cm). Fasten off.

MAKING UP
Join the two short ends using the crochet method.

TECHNIQUES USED

This project uses the following techniques:

Single crochet (UK double crochet) - *see page 18*

CIRCULAR THROW

Use this versatile throw to bring to life a chair or bed, adding texture and detail to a room.

MATERIALS

Rowan Kid Classic
7 x 1.76oz (50g) balls, or any
medium weight yarn

Photographed in
A Pumice 888 x 3
B Feather 828 x 3
C Bitter Sweet 866 x 1

Hook: US H8 (5mm)

GAUGE

10 stitches and 6 rows measure
4in (10cm) over pattern using
K10½ (6.5mm) crochet hook

FINISHED SIZE

Approximately 31½ x 31½in
(80 x 80cm)

Motif size 4½in (11½cm)
measured across.

CIRCULAR THROW

Make 49 circular motifs, each the same as follows.

Foundation chain: Using yarn A make six chains, join with
a slip stitch to form a ring.

Round 1: Make three chains – this counts as your first
double crochet (UK treble crochet). Work fifteen more
double crochets (UK treble crochet) into the ring. Join your
ring with a slip stitch into the third chain of your original
three chains.

Round 2: Make four chains – this counts as your first
double crochet (UK treble crochet) and one chain. *Work
one double crochet (UK treble crochet) into next double
crochet (UK treble crochet) from previous round, make one
chain. Repeat from * fourteen more times. Join with a slip
stitch into third chain of your original four chains.
Break off yarn A

Round 3: Join in yarn B to any double from the previous
round. Make three chains – this counts as your first double
crochet (UK treble crochet). *Work two double crochets
(UK treble crochet) into next chain space, one double
crochet (UK treble crochet) into next double crochet (UK
treble crochet). Repeat from * fourteen more times. Join with
a slip stitch into third chain of your original three chains.

Round 4: Make one chain. Work a single crochet
(UK double crochet) into each stitch of previous round.
Fasten off yarn B and join yarn C

Round 5: Join yarn C into any single crochet (UK double
crochet) from the previous round. Make one chain. Work
a single crochet (UK double crochet) into each stitch from
previous round. Fasten off.

MAKING UP
To join, place seven circles side by side in a row. Using
mattress stitch join each circle where it touches the next.
Repeat this step six more times. Lay each strip side by side,
join in same way where each circle touches.

STRIPED PILLOW

An eye-catching pillow, will make a wonderful feature in any room. Choose colours that complement your current room colour scheme, or opt for something a little different.

MATERIALS

Rowan Big Wool
4 x 3.5oz (100g) balls,
or any super bulky weight yarn

Photographed in
A Pantomime 079 x 2
B Yoke 078 x 1
C Burnt Orange 051 x 1

Hook: US O16 (12mm)

GAUGE

8 stitches and 9 rows measure 4in
(10cm) over pattern using
US O16 (12mm) crochet hook

FINISHED SIZE

15¾ x 15¾in (40 x 40cm). You will
need a pillow inside which is also
this size.

STRIPED PILLOW

Pattern note: This design is worked diagonally starting in the
bottom left corner.

FRONT PIECE
Make two chains with yarn A.

Row 1: Work two single crochet (UK double crochet) into
second chain from the hook. You should have two stitches.

Join in yarn B using slip stitch. Make one chain – this is your
turning chain. Turn your work.

Row 2: Work two single crochet (UK double crochet) into
both stitches. You should now have four stitches.

Make one chain and turn your work.

Row 3: Work two single crochets (UK double crochet) into the
first stitch, single crochet in each stitch to the last, work two
single crochets (UK double crochet) into the last stitch. You
should now have six stitches.

Join in yarn C. Make one chain and turn your work.

The last row sets the pattern, continue in pattern and
colour sequence until 14 rows have been worked in total.

Start of decreasing.

Row 31: Single crochet (UK double crochet) the first two
stitches together, single crochet (UK double crochet) in each
stitch of the row to the last two stitches, single crochet
(UK double crochet) two stitches together. Two stitches
have been decreased.

Repeat last row, keeping colour sequence until you have two
stitches remaining. Fasten off.

BACK PIECE
Work as for front piece until start of decreasing. Change to
yarn A. Continue in pattern while only using yarn A until you
have one stitch remaining. Fasten off.

MAKING UP

Join three sides using mattress stitch, insert pillow inside and join last edge together.

TECHNIQUES USED

This project uses the following techniques covered in the lessons:

Single crochet (UK double crochet) - *see page 18*

Increasing - *see page 27*

Decreasing - *see page 28*

Joining in a new yarn colour- *see page 26*

SIMPLE WRIST WARMERS

Wrap up for winter with these simple wrist warmers. Make them in several colours to complement your look, or opt for a neutral tone to wear with everything. Chunky and soft with a great texture stitch.

MATERIALS

Rowan Lima Colour
2 x 1.76oz (50g) balls, or any
medium weight yarn

Photographed in Nepal 716

Hook: US H8 (5mm)

GAUGE

14 stitches and 12 rows measure
4in (10cm) over half double pattern
using H8 (5mm) crochet hook

FINISHED SIZE

Circumference: 6½in (16½cm)
Length: 10½in (27cm)

SIMPLE WRIST WARMERS

Make two.

Make 40 chains.

Row 1: Work your first half double crochet (UK half treble)
into the third chain from the hook. Work a half double crochet
(UK treble crochet) into each stitch to complete your row.
You should have 37 stitches.

Make two chains – these are your turning chains.
Turn your work.

Row 2: Work the first half double crochet (UK treble crochet)
into the next stitch from the chain base. Complete your row
with half double crochet (UK half treble crochet).
Make two chains and turn.

Repeat the last row until your work measures 6½in
(16½cm). Fasten off.

MAKING UP
Join starting edge to finishing edge (long sides) with
mattress stitch.

TECHNIQUES USED

This project uses the following techniques:

Half double crochet (UK half treble crochet) -
see page 20

WITH THANKS

I would like to thank everybody who has helped me pull this book together. Most importantly, my wonderful husband, for putting up with all of the late nights I spent writing this book and supporting me in managing my time.

Special thanks also goes to Kate Buller and the team at Rowan for supporting my book with yarn sponsorship.

Finally, I would like to thank the team at Search Press and Quail for bringing my ideas to life and making this book possible.

Emma x

I just had to squeeze this photo in; my adorable Pomerainian puppy - Rupert. Holder of his very own Instagram account & lover of destroying balls of very expensive yarn!!

Horsham Township Library

Published in 2015 by
Search Press Ltd
Wellwood
North Farm Road
Tunbridge Wells
Kent, TN2 3DR
UK

ISBN: 978-1-78221-220-1

Conceived, designed and produced b
Quail Publishing
2/3 Black Horse Barns
Fancott
Toddington
Bedfordshire, LU5 6HT
UK

Art Editor: Georgina Brant
Designers: Quail Studio
Copy Editor: Katie Heppell
Photography: Quail Studio
Creative Director: Darren Brant
Yarn Support: Rowan Yarns

Printed in China